www.Jadubbenterprises.com

Self Help Quick Guides
How to Spot Authentic Designer Handbags

Table of Contents

Chanel

First of all, you have to look at the outside of the bag. Even a fake bag can give a very nice first impression, but if you look more carefully, you will be able to notice major differences. For example, the most common way to spot a fake Chanel is by the interlocking C logo.

The two C's have to be interlocked, not one above the other. Also, knockoffs tend to interlock O's which are later snipped so they can look like C's. You will notice the difference if you take a close look. And don't forget to check the quilting of the bag. Usually, in fake bags, the shape is wrong and the workmanship is just not clean. Authentic ones don't have a heavy quilting, it is always subtle and perfectly done.

It is always very easy to know if a Chanel bag is real or not just by looking at the quilting. You can see which one has over the top quality workmanship and which one does not.

A real Chanel bag will always come in its dust bag. Some fakes may have a dust bag but it is highly unlikely. Vintage Chanel bags will come in a white felt bag with a black logo, and newer designs in a black bag with a white logo.

Another one of the easiest ways to spot a fake Chanel is by looking at the back pocket. The fake's back pockets are bigger and the diamond quilt is not perfectly lined up like an original. The back pocket of an original Chanel will always look more subtle and look like a soft wave at the top edge, while fakes look like a flat curve.

Inside an original bag, it should deb stamped with CHANEL one the inside and 'Made in France' underneath it to the side. You can also look for the authenticity cards but they are often copied, so don't rely completely on the authenticity cards.

The most effective way of all is to check the two flaps of the bag. If you open the bag and check the first flap, it should be very smooth. The first flap of fake ones are usually not as smooth and very wrinkly as well. Then, go and look at the second flap. An authentic Chanel will always have the interlocking C's logo. Many fake ones have them too, but they are never quite like the logo. Many times they are either too skinny or too broad. But on the second flap you should also notice that the interlocking logo on authentic bags is raised a little bit. And on the contrary the knock-offs will be way too flat or raised too much.

Prada

Prada is one of the most desired brands of handbags. So it is pretty obvious that it is one of the brands that get faked the most. Fortunately, there are very simple ways to spot a fake or original Prada.

When you look at a Prada bag, the first thing you need to do is look at the exterior logo plaque. If it is an authentic, the color of the enamel should be the exact color of the bag or very close to it. And of course make sure it is in the shape of a triangle. If it is not a triangle or it is just the letters on the outside, it's fake.

The interior logo plaque of authentic Prada bags will depend on how old the bag is. It should read Prada Milano made in Italy in either one, two or three lines. If it doesn't say the entire phrase it's not original.

You should also check that the interior plaque matches the interior fabric of the bag. Sometimes, it is not a ceramic plaque, it can be a leather patch with four filled out rivets.

And there are the zippers. This is one of the easiest and fastest ways to spot a real Prada bag. You should be aware that Prada zippers are super smooth and you should be able to use them with no trouble at all. But the real catch in zippers is that Prada only uses certain types – or we could say brands – of zippers.

The following list will show the only zippers that Prada uses for their bags:
•Lampo
•Ykk

•Riri
•Opti
•Ipi

These names will be embossed on the back side of the zipper.
The hardware is another key factor. Every single Prada bag that is authentic will have Prada embossed on them, no matter if they are old or new. They will always have Prada on them whether they are buckles, locks, metal feet, or zippers.

Also take a look at the entire lining of the bag. If it is original, it should shave the word Prada all over the lining. But make sure they are written in a horizontal way, if not it is not authentic. But don't rely completely on the lining because sometimes the interior can be plain nylon and match the exterior of the handbag.

And last but not least, is this great and almost foolproof way to determine if a Prada bag is authentic or a knock off: the interior number tag. If you are not buying the bag online, look for a small and white tag in the interior, it will have a random number on it. You should look for it in the interior pocket of the bag. It will always be on that pocket. And if you are buying online, most reliable sellers will have a picture of the tag among the other pictures of the bag.

Louis Vuitton

This brand has existed for quite a while now, but still people haven't gotten tired of them. It is actually easy to spot a real or fake Louis Vuitton. First of all, you need to look at its price. You have to be realistic, if you find a "new" bag that costs less than $300 then it is probably a fake. You can't get a brand new Louis Vuitton at such a low price.

Also check for the price tag. Generally, the original bags will come with the tag in a pocket of the purse, and not attached on the outside. So check for the tag inside of the bag, also ignore all bags with cheap and flimsily attached tags.

You should also avoid all Louis Vuitton bags that have plastic wrapping over the handles. You should do this because the oxidizing cowhide leather does not need to be covered. Authentic Louis Vuitton bags –and all other top brands– do not have plastic on the handles.

If you are planning to buy the classic monogrammed bag, taking a very close look at the LV pattern is one of the best ways to spot fake and real Louis Vuitton. Only the real bags will have the letters printed in gold with fine brown lines. So you should completely avoid the ones with solid colored monograms and the ones with a green tint, they are complete knock- offs.

Then there is all of the clasps and hardware of the bag. Like any other high-end brand, Louis Vuitton only uses brass or gold metal for their clasps and hardware. Although many of the fake bags will have golden hardware, most of the times it is just plastic with a layer of gold paint, so watch out for that too.

And of course, original bags will have the "LV" or "Louis Vuitton" logo imprinted on the pull of the zipper. Be careful because many fake bags also have the imprinted logo, but you can always tell when it is real because it is a much more clean and precise imprinted logo.

What many look for first to see if Louis Vuitton is real is the "Made in" label. Originally, all the Louis Vuitton bags were made in France, but now the company produces bags in four more countries: United States, Italy, Spain and Germany. So don't discard a bag if you see a Made in label with any of those countries on it.

If you are not looking for a vintage Louis Vuitton, then looking for a date code is a good idea. Most of the bags after the early 1980s have a production code stamped on them.

Since the 1990's, the code includes two letters followed by four numbers. Before the 1990's, the code was a one or two letter code followed by three or four numbers. Some were also simple three number codes.

Coach

It is very easy to tell when a bag is fake, but especially Coach bags. There are a lot of factors that make a fake bag look like a total knock-off, but most people don't realize it. Once you are aware of those factors, you won't doubt the next time you see a Coach bag.

When it comes to the classic Coach pattern bag, the first thing that you have to do is inspect the CC pattern. In authentic Coach bags, the CC pattern is perfectly aligned in both the horizontal and the vertical way. You won't see just the half of a C because the seam went right over it in a real one.

Also, the edge of the horizontal "C" and the edge of the vertical "C" do not touch. In authentic Coach bags, the horizontal "C" touches its vertical counterpart. The pattern should also have two vertical and two horizontal rows of Cs, not one.

Then after checking the outside open the bag and look for the credo patch, ALL Coach bags have a leather patch sewn into the lining. In this patch, you must see a serial number stamped on it. Usually the serial number is a number-letter combination.

Don't forget to look at the zippers and fixtures either. But don't get confused, the zipper pull can be made of leather or a series of rings, but the zipper mechanism –which has the zipper pull attached to it– should be embossed with the letters YKK, which is a super high quality zipper manufacturer. The letters can be small and hard to see but they are there. It has been confirmed that not all authentic bags have those zippers. So don't leave the bag if it doesn't have the letters because it could be real, if it does then you can be sure it is.

And regarding the fixtures, the word COACH should be stamped on the majority of the metal hardware, but you should know that some of the newer models don't have the stamp on any of the nickel/brass hardware. So in this kind of situation the best thing you can do is check a reliable website and look at the authentic product and compare it with the bag you are looking at.

Now, it is common for people to think that when a Coach bag says "Made in China" it is a fake, since Coach bags are made in Italy. Actually if a bag says made in China it does not necessarily mean it is a fake. Newer models are made in China and other countries, but most of them –especially the classic ones– were made in Italy.

But the most obvious and easy way to know how if the bag is authentic, is simply where you are buying it. If you are at a department store then you don't even have to check the authenticity, but if you are buying one at a small shop that sells "authentic designer bags" then you should take your time to look at it.

Fendi

Spotting fake Fendi bags is not that complicated either. Since Fendi has been a very popular brand for decades, you can find plenty of knock-offs everywhere. But still, nobody can pull off the amazing quality and look of an original Fendi bag.

Like most of the other brands, one of the first things you should look at is the stitching of the bag. Every single one of the stitches should be perfectly straight with the one before it and the one after it, they can't be loose and the thread should match the material perfectly.

Then take a careful look at the logo. Many fake bags might have a label that is convincing, but an authentic Fend will be perfectly engraved into the leather and not printed on the surface of it.

Check all of the hardware of the bag, it should have the Fendi logo engraved. But don't assume that if the hardware is engraved it is automatically a real one. Many fakes have the logo engraved, but you can see the difference between a fake engraving and the clean and careful engraving of an authentic. Also make sure every piece of hardware has a cover on it because real Fendi bags have a cover that you can remove after purchasing it.

Open the bag and look inside for the authenticity card. They are usually made of leather but an authentic should always have one inside. Another key factor is the serial number. The serial number should be printed on the inside of the bag, particularly in Fendi bags, the serial number is just numbers and with no letters. It doesn't matter if the bag has everything a real bag has, if it does not have a serial number, leave it.

This next trick might sound weird, and you might look weird yourself doing it but it is worth it: sniff the bag. If you know what calfskin smells like, then that is the smell you should be looking for. Brand new Fendi bags smell like calfskin, while knock-offs usually smell like cheap material and chemicals.

And if you are buying a brand new bag – this can and should happen with used ones– it should come with its own dust bag. Although there is not just one design for Fendi dust bags, it should have the word Fendi on it and sometimes the logo too. Look at pictures of Fendi dust bags online and compare it with the dust bag of the handbag you are buying – especially if you are buying a used one online.

One of the things that Fendi has put more effort into is to make their products as hard to copy as possible, so to do this they came up with the hologram sticker. The hologram sticker is encoded and it can only be seen with a special magnifying device. It doesn't get easier than that.

Gucci

Gucci bags have multiple, very specific factors that make them easily recognizable. For example, when buying a Gucci bag you should look for the 'Controllato Card'. The Controllato Card always accompanies Gucci bags, and it signifies that the bag was checked after it was made.

The word GUCCI should be printed big and in the center of the card, with the word controllato beneath it in a smaller size. And beneath the word controllato should a set of numbers 1234567890.

Brand new Gucci bags always come with their own dust bag – and usually used ones too if you are buying them online. Gucci dust bags come in many different styles and colors, but some of the most common styles are: black and brown with the GG logo repeated all over it; brown, with a drawstring and the word GUCCI in a golden color; dark brown, and GUCCI in gold.

Original Gucci bags don't only come with the Controllato Card, they also come with an information booklet. Look at all of it carefully, the logo the spacing of the word GUCCI, and even for spelling errors which obviously only fake bags will have – though it is rare to find knock offs that come with the booklet.

The booklet and card are not the only things that should come with the bag, there is one more card you should look for, the Firenze Card. The card should say GUCCI in the middle and Firenze 1921 in small font on the bottom. So enough with the printed cards and booklets, you should start looking at the actual bag. New Gucci handbags have a label inside of them.

This label should include the words GUCCI and made in Italy as well as the registered trademark circled R.

Then there is also the serial number. The serial number comes on the reverse of the label, usually the sequence is two sets of numbers one above the other but it can vary. If there is no serial number on the bag, then you must know it is definitively a fake.

Of course you should take a look at the hardware too, which should be solid metal and most of the pieces must be engraved carefully and cleanly with the word Gucci.

Also take your time looking at the stitches of the bag. The stitching on original Gucci bags is perfect and without a single flaw. It is straight, neat and completely even.

And if the one you are planning to buy is one with the double GG logo on the exterior then you should know that the G on the left has to be facing forward, and the G on the right has to be facing backwards. Remember that it is the brand's logo, so any minimal mistakes in the consistency or spacing is the deal breaker.

And finally, the code tag. New Gucci bags have a code tag in their interior. The tag comes with a QR type code and the word Gucci. But once again, only the newer models come with this tag.

Michael Kors

Michael Kors has become one of the most popular designers when it comes to affordable luxury, and especially in bags. So it is no surprise that you can find knock-offs of this brand everywhere. But with the following tips it won't be hard to recognize them.

First of all, when you are looking at a bag pay close attention to the leather. Specifically newer models – like the Selma bag – are made of Saffiano leather. This kind of leather is dense and rigid, and the texture is clearly in a very small criss-cross/diagonal pattern. It is also waxed so you will notice a semi gloss.

Don't forget to look at the hardware of the bag too. Usually in Michael Kors bags, the hardware has a small hint of copper tone. The buckles of authentic bags are mostly rounded squares and are flat along the edges, while fakes usually are simple rounded hoops.

And you must look at the zippers and closure of the bag as well. Real Michael Kors bags have zipper pulls with the words MICHAEL KORS engraved cleanly and perfectly on them. Knock offs will most likely have the MK logo made of metallic covered plastic. Also open and close the zipper a few times, a real bag will open and close very smoothly, and fake ones will get stuck and won't close and open as smoothly.

Then you have the handle or handles of the bag. The handles of real bags will be stiff and tight, on the contrary, handles of fake bags tend to be filled with a foam tube which will make the top part of the handle look pleated and overall flimsy.

After that, open the bag. Original bags always come with a care card. You can find this care card inside the interior pocket of the bag. It will tell you the materials the bag is made of and how to take care of it. Although many fakes might have this card, not all of them do, so if the one you want doesn't have the card, it is certainly a fake. Be very careful and look thoroughly at the stitching. It should be in a straight line, evenly-spaced and done very neatly. The thread of a real one will never be of a contrasting color, it will always be as similar to the color of the bag as possible.

On the interior of the bag you will also find a tag that says where the bag was made. Older designs will say made in the United States, but newer models are made in China and some other countries like Korea, Indonesia, and Vietnam, so any of those are good.

In that same tag, you should find a series of letters and numbers. This series represent the style of the bag. It is very important that you look for this tag because if the bag doesn't have it, then it is not an authentic Michael Kors bag.

Burberry

Everyone knows that no matter what, Burberry is always going to be one of the –if not the– top luxury brand of all. Their designs have survived the test of time and people don't seem to ever get tired of them, and so do counterfeits.

When you purchase a brand new Burberry bag –as well as online– it will come with its own dust bag. Although there is no specific style for Burberry dust bags, the brand tends to go for a black or cream bag with the logo and BURBERRY established in 1856 in cream or black respectively.

Before you buy it, you should look inside of it and see if it comes with a booklet. The newer models always come with a booklet with the Burberry logo on the front. The booklet usually says how to take care of the bag and the materials it is made of in multiple languages.

You should also open it to check that there is a label or stamp stitched onto the bag, usually beneath the zipper of the inner pocket. If the bag does not have the label or stamp with the word BURBERRY on it, then you can be sure it is not an authentic bag.

Inside you should also find another label, but this one is attached to the lining. Burberry bags are made in China, Italy and Romania, so it is okay if the label says made in with any of those three countries. After you find that label, check its reverse. For it to be a real Burberry bag, the reverse must have a series of numbers and letters. The series represents the particular style of that bag. Once again, if there is no label or it does not include the made in or the serial number, it is not authentic.

Newer models also come with a swing tag on the outside. The tag must have the logo or the word BURBERRY. If it is the latter, analyze the font carefully, if there is wrong-spacing or anything of the sort. But be careful not to rely completely on this because many knock offs can come with original swing tags.

On the inside of the swing tag there should be details about that specific bag, like its color and the style as well as a barcode. Make sure that the information that comes on the swing tag matches the bag. And regarding the hardware, all of it will be made of solid metal and it will not flake or chip, ever. Bigger pieces can be engraved with the logo and it will have a clean and perfect finish.

Finally there is the stitching of the bag. Like any other luxury brand, the stitching of a real Burberry bag will be perfect and flawless. It will be straight, won't be loose, it will be completely even and clean and not at all sloppy or badly aligned.

Jimmy Choo

Although Jimmy Choo is most known for its gorgeous –and quite expensive– shoes, the brand is also brilliant when it comes to designing bags. Jimmy Choo might not be the top brand when it comes to counterfeits, you can end up stumbling upon some really good knock offs.

If you are not sure if it is original or not, the first thing you should look for is the inside label. It is one of the easiest and quickest ways to spot fakes. The inside label is stitched to the interior and is always made of metal and of a lilac color; look online so you can recognize the right lilac color because any imitations can have a very similar tone. Also, it should have a leather backing and the letters must be gold or silver.

Then also look at the lining of the bag. Specifically on the models Ramona and Riki (the most counterfeited ones), their linings are a tan moleskin color. Imitations will often have suede or satin linings and try to match the natural color of the real ones.

And remember the hardware too. Authentic Jimmy Choo hardware is big and quite unique. The locking system of the bag will be substantially heavy, meanwhile most knock offs will feel light or not heavy enough. Then, the zipper of the inside pocket will always match the color of the bag perfectly as well as being engraved with the words JIMMY CHOO.

Inspect the font. With some of the better knockoffs, the difference may only be noticeable in the lettering details. In the two MM's in JIMMY, the first line of each M should be very thin.

The horizontal crossbar of the H in CHOO should be toward the top rather than in the center of the letter. The O's in CHOO should appear to be slightly dented, and more oval in shape rather than perfect circles.

Also check the screws of the bag. The screws of real Jimmy Choo bags will be flat head screws, but they will never be phillips head. On the metal clasp, the letter has to be centered in both a horizontal and vertical way.

You should also be sure that the bag comes with its own dust bag. The Jimmy Choo bags will come with a purple dust bag that says Made in Italy. They will never be white, tan, black, brown or any other color. Another thing you should be sure of is that the bag has an authenticity card. Fake bags will usually have it outside and proudly hanging from the bag to try to persuade you. Most luxury bags, no matter the brand, have their authenticity card inside one of the inner pockets.

But most importantly, before even inspecting the bag you should think about the price. Be rational and reasonable, you will not find a real Jimmy Choo bag for less than several -- meaning seven or eight -- hundreds of dollars, not even the used and old ones, are that much less than a brand new bag.

Marc Jacobs

During the past years, Marc Jacobs has become one of the most popular designers in the world. Above all, what people are most attracted to from his collections are his bags. He has very original and unique taste, which more often than not is counterfeited.

When trying to authenticate a Marc Jacobs bag, check first the most important parts that make a bag a quality one. For instance, the zippers. Look at the underside of the zipper lock, all authentic Marc Jacobs bags will have the word Riri engraved on it. If it does not say that, it is definitively a fake.

But sometimes, replicas can have Riri engraved too, but usually you will find the engraving not as clean and precise. Also, if you are not sure about it, check the official Marc Jacobs website and look for the same bag. Check the shape of the zippers and see if they match the ones on the bag.

The next thing you should look at is the handles of the bag. Replicas tend to have plastic wraps covering the handles because the material is cheap and it can get easily damaged. Authentic purses are never wrapped in any sort of plastic.

You should also open the bag to see if on the inside is a metal label. The metal label should read "Marc Jacobs". Don't fall for a bag that has a leather or fabric tag. If it doesn't have a metal label, or no label at all, it's a fake.

While you are checking out the inside of the bag, you should also look for the serial number. The serial number comes in a tag that is attached to the lining. This serial number can include both numbers and letters. Just like the metal label, if there's no serial number, it's not authentic.

Inside of the bag, there should also be a care card. Care cards only come in the newer models and the content of the card can vary depending on the type and style of the bag. Just like there is a care card inside, there should also be a little booklet.

The booklet usually contains information about the materials the bag is made of, details about the proper care of the bag among other things and in multiple languages like English, Spanish, French and Italian.

Coming back to the outside, the newest models will come with a swing tag. The swing tag of a bag will detail all of the information of the bag, its style, its color and will also have a barcode on it. But you should not rely solely on the swing tag because many replicas can come with an original swing tag. And obviously, make sure that the description of the swing tag matches the bag.

Finally, take your time to look and feel the leather of the bag. Marc Jacobs bags only use high quality leather, so if it feels cheap, a little too stiff or a little too flimsy, don't buy it.

Chloe

Chloe is another one of those brands that are never out of style. They have a lot of different designs from years ago that people still use today. So, it is not a surprise that replica makers try to take advantage of these beautiful bags.

Since Chloe bags don't have a specific pattern or logo like the MK from Michael Kors or the Cs from Coach, it can be easier to get confused by look-alikes. But, paying attention to detail, it won't be that hard to recognize an original.

When you look at a Chloe bag, whether it is online or in person, look at the stitching. Most Chloe bags use a thick nylon thread for the stitching, which makes it tight and straight. You will never see a Chloe bag with loose and uneven stitching made with a thin thread.

Next, look at the handles of the bag. Authentic Chloe bags have an extra piece of leather around the top of the strap, so the seam should be pointed outwards. The seam of fake bags will point towards each other or towards the center. Also, the stitching on the handle should be of thick nylon thread, tight and even.

Moving on to the Chloe logo and the lock, if the logo is on top of a keyhole that is upside down, then it is certain that the bag is not authentic. A real Chloe bag will have the wide part of the keyhole facing the logo.

There is also the overall metal of the bag. The lock, rivets and key should all be of the exact same color. Usually, the color is a dark antique brushed brass tone, but it can vary. A fake Chloe bag will have different colors on the lock, rivets and keys as well as not being actual metal, just metallic colored plastic that will chip with time.

Though this tip is very helpful, most times it's hard to do; but you should weigh the bag. Yes, if you have the chance to weigh it, because a real Chloe bag always weighs more than 1.36kg pounds. If you can't weigh it just carry it and guess its weight. But only rely on the obvious fact that if it is very light then it is a fake.

Going back to hardware, look at the zipper of the bag. Besides the fact that it should be silver, some of them have the letters YKK engraved on them. This is mostly to ensure that it is real, because some Chloe bags don't have that engraving and they are original.

And If sellers say it is a "Factory Second", it is a fake. There is no such thing as a Factory Second. A "Power Seller" does not guarantee genuineness. "Power Seller" simply means, they sell a lot on the market. Selling a lot has nothing to do with authenticity.

Hermes

The first thing that makes original Hermes bags stand out is their posture. Yes, their posture. A real one will stand up straight and tall, you will never see one slouching back and if you do, that's when you know it's a fake, you don't even have to look at it up close.

Then if you want to be super sure check the linings. Go to the online page of Hermes and look at the color of the lining of the bag that you want. Not a similar bag, the exact same one– since the color varies depending on the style. Many Hermes bags come in bold and not very common colors so don't assume it is a fake.

The stamp of approval is another good option to check the authenticity of the bag. Between the clasp and the bag's opening should be the Hermes stamp. The stamp has to say Hermes Paris – Made in France. Some replicas have the stamp too, but it ends up flaking off so take a close look.

Another key factor is the hardware. You will always see very fine, delicate, and clean engravings on their hardware. For instance, the clasp of the bag should have HERMES - PARIS engraved on it. Usually the engraving of knock offs are not as neat, they are deeper and the letters are chunkier.

There is also a more discrete detail on the right strap of the bag: an I.D. Check, it is tucked on the reverse side of the strap. The code is a letter and number combination.

And whether you are buying in person or online, ask to see the dust bag of the bag. Any bag –especially if it's new– has to come with its own dust bag. Unlike the dust bags of many other designers, the Hermes dust bag is popular for always being of an orange color.
Also pay very close attention to the stitching. It is known that all Hermes bags are hand-stitched, so you must know that the stitching is

not going to be perfect and uniform. Replicas are stitched by machines, so if the bag is super and completely straight, it is not original. It is very easy for one to recognize when something came straight from a factory and when it was made by hand. Plus the stitching of fakes won't stay together for long.

And once again, unlike many other designer bags, Hermes bags don't come with an authenticity card. Many times replica makers make authenticity cards for all brands to convince people that they are originals, so don't get fooled by this.

Finally, there's the price. If you find a price that is just too good to be true, then it probably is. Think it through, a brand new Hermes can cost $18,000 and sometimes more. The cheapest price you could stumble upon if you are lucky could be around $6,500. So don't get your hopes up if you find one that is not close to that, chances are it is not an original.

www.ingramcontent.com/pod-product-compliance
Lightning Source LLC
Chambersburg PA
CBHW051421130726
47989CB00007B/3021